California

BY MARI KESSELRING

The Child's World

Published by The Child's World®
1980 Lookout Drive • Mankato, MN 56003-1705
800-599-READ • www.childsworld.com

ACKNOWLEDGMENTS
The Child's World®: Mary Berendes, Publishing Director
The Design Lab: Design and production
Red Line Editorial: Editorial direction

PHOTO CREDITS: iStockphoto, cover, 1, 3; Matt Kania/Map Hero, Inc., 4,
5; Shutterstock Images, 7; Galina Barskaya/iStockphoto, 9; Laure Neish/
iStockphoto, 10; Jim Lopes/iStockphoto, 11; Felix Alim/iStockphoto, 13;
Photolibrary, 15; Brett Hillyard/iStockphoto, 17; Charles Sykes/AP Images,
19; Shutterstock Images, 21; One Mile Up, 22; Quarter-dollar coin image
from the United States Mint, 22

LIBRARY OF CONGRESS CATALOGING-IN-PUBLICATION DATA
Kesselring, Mari.
  California / by Mari Kesselring.
    p. cm.
  Includes bibliographical references and index.
  ISBN 978-1-60253-449-0 (library bound : alk. paper)
  1. California—Juvenile literature. I. Title.

F861.3.K47 2010
979.4—dc22

2010016147

Printed in the United States of America in Mankato, Minnesota.
July 2010
F11538

On the cover:
The Golden
Gate Bridge in
San Francisco
is 8,981 feet
(2,737 m) long.

CONTENTS

Geography

Let's explore California! California is in the western United States. The Pacific Ocean is to the west. California shares its southern border with Mexico. California is the third-largest state.

OREGON

IDAHO

UTAH

NEVADA

Eureka •

• Redding

Sacramento River

Santa Rosa •
Petaluma •

★
Sacramento

San Francisco •

• San
Jose

• Madera

• Monterey

NORTH
WEST EAST
SOUTH

CALIFORNIA

ARIZONA

Pacific
Ocean

Santa Barbara •

• Pasadena
Los Angeles •
• Anaheim

San Juan •

San Diego •

MEXICO

Cities

California has several cities that are among the biggest in the United States. Sacramento is the capital of California. Los Angeles is the largest city in the state. San Francisco, San Jose, and San Diego are other large cities in California.

Sacramento was named after the Sacramento River, ▶ which is near the city.

Land

California has forests, mountains, valleys, and deserts. The San Andreas **Fault** is in California. A fault is a break in Earth's crust. **Earthquakes** happen along the San Andreas Fault.

Northern California has many hills and valleys. ▶

Plants and Animals

The California state tree is the California redwood. California redwoods are the tallest trees in the world. They usually grow 200 to 300 feet (61–91 m) tall. The poppy is the state flower. It has golden yellow **petals**. The California quail is the state bird.

Hiking in the California redwood forests is a **popular** activity. ▶

The trunks of California redwoods are about 8 to 12 feet (2.4–3.7 m) wide.

People and Work

More than 30 million people live in California. This is more than in any other state. Many people work with **technology**. California has many farms, too. The state is also well known as a center for movies and television shows.

Silicon Valley is an area in California that is famous for creating computer parts.

California is one of the largest makers of computers in the world. ▶

History

Native Americans were the first people to live in the area that is now California. In the late 1600s, people from Spain began settling in the area. Mexico later owned the land. The United States bought the land from Mexico in 1848 after a war between the two countries. California became the thirty-first state on September 9, 1850.

People panned for gold in California in the 1800s. ▶

California's state nickname is "the Golden State." That is because gold was found in California in 1848. This led thousands of people to the area in search of gold. The event was called the "gold rush."

Ways of Life

In some parts of California, people enjoy outdoor activities all year long. With its long coastline, California has many beaches that people visit. **Surfing** is popular, too.

A surfer rides a wave on the Pacific Ocean in California. ▶

Famous People

Actors Zac Efron, Cameron Diaz, Carrie Fisher, and Will Ferrell were born in California. Football player Tom Brady and baseball player Barry Bonds were also born in this state.

Zac Efron acted in the *High School Musical* movies. ▶

Famous Places

California has many exciting places to see. Disneyland is one popular place. People also like to visit the Golden Gate Bridge in San Francisco. California also has many **theaters** that show plays.

Many people visit Los Angeles to explore Hollywood, ▶
which is a center for television and movies.

State Symbols

Seal

Minerva, the Roman goddess of wisdom, is on the California state seal. Go to childsworld.com/links for a link to California's state Web site, where you can get a firsthand look at the state seal.

Flag

A grizzly bear is on the California state flag. It is the state animal.

Quarter

The California state quarter shows John Muir, a writer who lived in California. The quarter came out in 2005.

Glossary

earthquakes (URTH-kwayks): Earthquakes are sudden, violent shakings caused by shifting in Earth's crust. Earthquakes are common in California.

fault (FAWLT): A fault is a large crack in Earth's crust. The San Andreas Fault is a fault in California.

hiking (HYK-ing): Hiking is taking a walk in a natural area, such as a hill or a mountain. Many people enjoy hiking in the forests of California.

petals (PET-ulz): Petals are the colorful parts of flowers. The poppy, California's state flower, has golden yellow petals.

popular (POP-yuh-lur): To be popular is to be enjoyed by many people. Los Angeles is a popular place to visit.

seal (SEEL): A seal is a symbol a state uses for government business. The California seal has the Roman goddess of wisdom on it.

surfing (SURF-ing): Surfing is riding big waves on a long board. Surfing is popular in California.

symbols (SIM-bulz): Symbols are pictures or things that stand for something else. The state seal and flag are California's symbols.

technology (tek-NAWL-uh-jee): Technology is scientific knowledge applied to practical things. Some people in California work in technology.

theaters (THEE-ih-turz): Theaters are buildings where movies and plays are shown. California has many theaters.

Further Information

Books

Domeniconi, David. *G is for Golden: A California Alphabet*. Chelsea, MI: Sleeping Bear Press, 2002.

Downey, Tika. *California: The Golden State*. New York: PowerKids Press, 2010.

Ryan, Pam Muñoz. *Our California*. Watertown, MA: Charlesbridge Publishing, 2008.

Web Sites

Visit our Web site for links about California: *childsworld.com/links*

Note to Parents, Teachers, and Librarians: We routinely verify our Web links to make sure they are safe and active sites. So encourage your readers to check them out!

Index